# CONTENTS

D0109529

*We dedicate this book to our grandmothers,
who instilled a love of jewelry in each of us
by letting us play in their jewelry boxes.*

# — BEADED JEWELRY —
# STRINGING
# TECHNIQUES

### Skills, Tools, and Materials for Making
### Handcrafted Jewelry

**Carson Eddy, Rachael Evans, and Kate Feld**

Storey Publishing

*The mission of Storey Publishing is to serve our customers by
publishing practical information that encourages
personal independence in harmony with the environment.*

Edited by Deborah Balmuth and Lisa H. Hiley
Series and cover design by Alethea Morrison
Art direction by Jeff Stiefel
Text production by Theresa Wiscovitch
Indexed by Christine R. Lindemer, Boston Road Communications

Cover illustration by © Caitlin Keegan
Interior illustrations by © Kate Feld

**Storey Publishing**
210 MASS MoCA Way
North Adams, MA 01247
*www.storey.com*

Printed in the United States by McNaughton & Gunn, Inc.
10 9 8 7 6 5 4 3 2 1

LIBRARY OF CONGRESS CATALOGING-IN-PUBLICATION DATA

Eddy, Carson.
  Beaded jewelry. Stringing techniques : skills, tools, and materials for making hand crafted jewelry / Carson Eddy, Rachael Evans, and Kate Feld.
     pages cm. — (A Storey basics title)
  Includes index.
  ISBN 978-1-61212-482-7 (pbk. : alk. paper) — ISBN 978-1-61212-483-4 (ebook)
  1. Beadwork. 2. Jewelry making. I. Evans, Rachael, 1980- II. Feld, Kate, 1982- III. Storey Publishing. IV. Title. V. Title: Stringing techniques.
TT860.E286 2014
745.594'2—dc23
                                    2014028193

# INTRODUCTION

Beautiful beads and the desire to adorn ourselves inspire us to learn how to make beaded bracelets and necklaces. Beads are made from every imaginable material and are distinguished from other ornamentation by the fact that they have a hole in them for stringing. Just about anything that can have a hole drilled through it can be a bead.

In addition to beads, other elements involved in making beaded jewelry include stringing materials, findings, and clasps. This book is designed as an easy reference guide to help you learn a new vocabulary and teach you the basics of stringing beaded jewelry.

Selecting beads that you love is always the best way to begin! Beads come in a nearly endless array of materials, colors, shapes, sizes, and finishes, which can make shopping for beads in a bead shop, at a bead show, or on the Internet a little overwhelming. Shopping in person is always best. You can select beads that are beautiful to look at, feel nice against the skin, and work well together in jewelry designs. Small, independently owned bead shops, unlike big box stores or the Internet, are staffed by knowledgeable jewelry makers who are usually an excellent resource.

Together we bring over 40 years of experience as bead buyers, jewelry makers, and lovers of beads to this book. Over the years we have learned that encouraging the mastery of basic jewelry-making skills has been the key to success for our customers and students. We also believe that being knowledgeable about beads and jewelry-making supplies is very important. We hope you will find this book useful and will keep it as a handy reference for many years to come.

*Carson, Rachael, and Kate*

# CHAPTER ONE

# BEAD BASICS

If you have been inspired to make your own beaded jewelry, you may be wondering where to begin. Learning as much as you can about beads, stringing materials, and jewelry-making components is a great place to start. In addition to knowing about the many different sizes, shapes, and styles of beads that you can work with, it is useful to learn about jewelry styles and how jewelry is constructed.

It is particularly useful to develop an understanding of how beads are grouped and categorized. In most cases, they are grouped in overlapping categories that include shape and size, hole size and drill style, and material and surface treatment. Learning to recognize how beads are crafted, manufactured, or cut is also helpful when evaluating the cost of beads and determining if you are paying a fair price.

# BEAD SIZES

Beads come in a vast array of sizes, allowing the jewelry maker to create a wide range of jewelry styles. Bead size may be determined by a particular manufacturing technique or by the material being drilled, formed, or extruded; or it may simply be the aesthetic of the bead maker. Beads are generally sized in millimeters, with basic round beads starting at 2 millimeters and ranging to 20 millimeters on up. Shaped beads come in a wide range of dimensions as well.

## Conversion Charts

Because beads are sold in millimeter dimensions and jewelry is frequently designed in inches, being able to quickly convert inches into millimeters and millimeters into inches is useful. The following charts are a quick reference for easily converting dimensions.

| English (Inches) to Metric (Millimeters) | | |
|---|---|---|
| WHEN YOU KNOW | MULTIPLY BY | TO FIND |
| Inches | 25 | Millimeters |
| Inches | 2.5 | Centimeters |
| Feet | 30 | Centimeters |
| Yards | .9 | Meters |

| Metric (Millimeters) to English (Inches) | | |
| --- | --- | --- |
| **WHEN YOU KNOW** | **DIVIDE BY** | **TO FIND** |
| Millimeters | 25 | Inches |
| Centimeters | 2.5 | Inches |
| Centimeters | 30 | Feet |
| Meters | .9 | Yards |

# BEAD SHAPES

THE LIST OF BEAD SHAPES is nearly endless, and new shapes are being developed all the time. By far the most common bead shape is round or spherical. Other shapes fall loosely into three overlapping categories — dimensional, geometric, and drop.

In addition to round beads, other basic dimensional shapes include barrels, bicones, cubes, dice, rondelles, saucers, and tubes. Organically shaped dimensional beads include chips, nuggets, and pebbles.

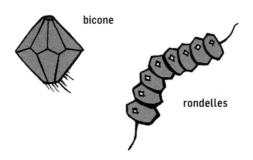

bicone

rondelles

Basic geometric bead shapes include coins, hexagons, octagons, ovals, rectangles, and squares. Common bead drop shapes include daggers, teardrops, and briolettes. Briolettes are traditionally defined as pear-shaped, faceted drops with a tip drill, but bead vendors and beaders refer to all gemstone drops (faceted and unfaceted) with a tip drill or front drill as briolettes (see Drill Styles, page 8). Other shapes include teardrop, onion, and heart.

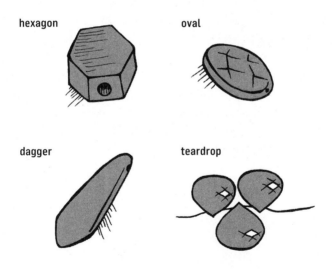

hexagon

oval

dagger

teardrop

To make this list even longer, many of these bead shapes also come in cut, flat, window-paned, puffed, or twisted versions. Regardless of shape, the color and other special qualities of a bead material are best showcased by a smooth surface. For added dimension and sparkle, beads may be cut or manufactured with a faceted surface. Facets are little cuts on the sides of beads. Both smooth and faceted beads come in a wide range of sizes.

# BEAD HOLES

WHATEVER MATERIAL THEY are made of, beads can be drilled with a range of bead hole sizes and in a number of different directions. The size of a bead hole and the drill style inform the choice of stringing material for a particular project. Bead hole size and drill style also determine how a single bead or a set of beads will sit or hang when strung. It is always important to consider bead hole size and drill style when selecting beads for particular beaded necklace or bracelet projects.

## Tech Tip
*When the beads in a project have different holes sizes, match the diameter of the stringing material to the bead with the smallest hole. If the beads all have large holes, try using a large diameter stringing material, multiple strands of cording, or spacer beads with smaller holes to get the project to hang correctly.*

Bead hole size corresponds directly to stringing material diameter. Bead hole sizes range from .05 millimeter in a tiny gemstone, pearl, or seed bead to over 4 millimeters in a large-hole bead. The most common bead hole sizes are from 1 to 2 millimeters.

When you are planning a project, start with selecting the beads. It is always a good idea to choose ones with similarly sized holes. If there is a noticeable difference in bead hole size, you can use spacer beads and bead caps to mask some of the variations, but if the variation is too great, the beads will not lie smoothly next to one another on the stringing material. Once you have selected all the beads for a project, you can decide what the most appropriate stringing material is.

If you want to use a particular stringing material, it is important to choose beads that fit snugly, though not too tightly, on the stringing material. If a bead with a large hole is strung on a small diameter stringing material, it will sag and not hang nicely when worn.

## Drill Styles

Beads are frequently described by how they are drilled. Round beads are most commonly drilled through the center, while other shapes may be drilled in a variety of directions. For example, a flat, rectangular bead may be center drilled through either the length or the width of the bead. It may also be drilled diagonally through the width at one end of the bead, or from front to back. These last variations in drill style add dimension to any jewelry project; they also allow a bead to be transformed into a pendant.

Most pressed or molded beads are machine drilled, making the resulting bead holes very consistent in diameter. Many natural materials, such as gemstones and pearls, are drilled by hand, which creates more irregular holes. Hand-drilled beads are most commonly drilled halfway from one side of the bead to the center, and then halfway from the other side to the center. This method of drilling often produces a drill hole that is wider on the surface and narrower in the center, which can pose problems when stringing (see Tech Tip below for how to use a bead reamer).

**bead reamer**

## Tech Tip

*If the holes in your beads are uneven or very small, use a bead reamer to try to enlarge the problematic holes. Select a bit for the bead reamer that matches the size of the hole you are working on. Insert the bit into each side of the bead and twist gently until the hole is large enough to string easily. Rough- or sharp-edged bead holes that may cut stringing material can also be smoothed out using a bead reamer.*

**Center drill** is the most common drill style. These beads are generally round or dimensional and are drilled through the center of the bead at its widest point.

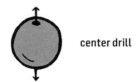

center drill

**Side drill** is another common style used with beads that are flat, square, or shaped. The hole runs from side to side at the widest point.

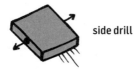

side drill

**Top drill** is used for beads with a definite top and bottom. This style of bead is drilled from top to bottom and they are often strung on wire or head pins to create dangles. *Vertical drill* is another style of top drill used when directionality is important. This style of bead may have a design or words on it that require the drill hole to run perpendicular.

top drill

**Front drill** is used for beads with a definite front and back. This style of bead is often turned into a charm or pendant by simply adding a jump ring or split ring through the drill hole.

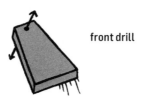

front drill

**Tip drill** is used for beads that have a distinct top and bottom but no definite front or back. This style of bead is drilled through the top of the bead and will hang like a pendant or can be strung to hang side by side.

tip drill

**Diagonal drill** refers to any square, cube, or rectangular bead that is drilled from corner to corner. These beads hang on the diagonal when strung.

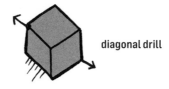

diagonal drill

**Double drill** refers to any bead that has two parallel holes. This style of bead may be drilled with centered, side-by-side holes or with holes at the top and bottom. This drill style helps the beads to lie flat or to function as spacer bars (see page 49) in a multistrand project.

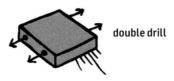

double drill

## BEAD MATERIALS

THE OLDEST KNOWN BEADS WERE crafted by early humans from marine shells over 100,000 years ago. The use of beads for body decoration and jewelry is a distinctly modern human trait. There is no evidence that Neanderthals, the predessors of modern humans, made beads or used personal adornment of any kind.

Today, beads are made from a huge variety of materials using a wide range of techniques. Gemstones are cut by hand, and pearls are cultured on pearl farms. Other natural materials like wood, horn, and bone are carved or shaped either by hand or by machine. Some beads are handcrafted or manufactured from molten glass, ceramic, porcelain, and precious metals. Beads are also pressed or molded from a wide range of pliable materials like plastic and resin. Found objects like nuts, seeds, teeth, and antlers are transformed into beads with carefully placed drill holes. Some of the most common bead materials are described in the following sections.

# GLASS BEADS

GLASS BEADS ARE CATEGORIZED BY the method used to manipulate molten glass to create the beads. Today, manufactured beads are usually drawn, pressed, or molded while handcrafted glass beads are lamp worked, blown, or cast. Different glass composites create different colors, metallic coatings and linings add interest, and the skill of the bead maker always adds value. Types of glass beads include the following.

**Drawn glass beads** are produced by pulling molten glass in such a way that a bubble is maintained in the center of a long cane of glass. The cane is then chopped into individual slices and rolled in hot sand to smooth the edges. Tiny seed beads are manufactured using highly sophisticated machines that mechanically draw (or extrude), chop, and smooth the beads. Different brands of seed beads are produced on different machinery. Each brand of seed beads has a signature shape — some are rounder, some are more donut shaped, and others are slightly irregular.

**Pressed and molded glass** beads are made from thick rods of molten glass that are fed into elaborate presses or molds that form the glass and pierce the hole. The freshly pressed or molded glass beads are then rolled in hot sand to reduce the seam lines. Glass beads pressed and molded in the Czech

Republic have long been the world's finest. They are the result of superior bead stamps and molds, as well as centuries of glass-making experience.

**Lampwork beads** are handcrafted from canes of colored glass that are worked around a metal rod over a specialized lampworking torch. After the beads are formed and decorated, they are fired in a kiln to anneal (harden) the glass. The type of glass used, the type and temperature of torch used, and the skill of the artist determine the quality and price of lampwork beads.

**Dichroic beads** are lampwork or pressed glass beads that have been fused with a thin coating of metal to create a color-changeable surface with a high sheen.

**Furnace glass beads** are made from decorative canes of glass encased in clear glass that is extruded, cut into beads, and fired or annealed in a furnace to strengthen the glass.

**Sand-cast beads**, also called powder glass beads or recycled glass beads, are primarily made in West Africa, though many Chinese reproductions have entered the marketplace recently.

Traditionally, these beads are made from broken beads, broken bottles, and other glass leftovers. The glass is ground, heated, and poured into hand-formed clay molds, and then pierced to make the hole before firing. The beads are fired over a carefully tended wood fire. The low temperature of the wood fire gives the beads their unique texture. Once the beads have cooled, they are released from the molds, washed to reveal the color, and in some cases, painted with designs.

# CRYSTAL BEADS

CRYSTAL BEADS ARE MADE FROM leaded glass. Lead is added to the normal ingredients of glass, which include quartz sand, soda, potash, and other minerals. The addition of lead to a traditional glass recipe adds weight, improves durability, and increases the prismatic qualities of the glass. The amount of lead used in glass crystal varies from brand to brand. Although lead can be a toxic substance if consumed, wearing leaded crystal jewelry does not pose a health risk.

**Swarovski Crystal**, made in Austria, is the finest brand of crystal on the market. Swarovski beads and pendants have a 32 percent lead content, which makes them the heaviest and most prismatic of the crystal beads manufactured today.

In 1895 Daniel Swarovski, who was born in northern Bohemia (now the Czech Republic), developed a highly specialized glass-cutting machine that transformed the crystal-cutting industry. Swarovski beads are unique not only because of their high lead content, but also because of the proprietary precision-cutting techniques that the company has perfected over more than a century.

**Preciosa crystal** is made by Jablonex, the centuries-old Bohemian (now Czech) manufacturer of cut glass and chandelier components. In addition to glass components and crystal beads, Jablonex manufactures seed beads and pressed and molded glass beads. Preciosa crystal has a 30 percent lead content, which makes it similar in weight to Swarovski Crystal. The real difference between Swarovski and Preciosa crystal can be seen in the cut, with the resulting prismatic qualities of the beads and pendants.

**Glass crystal** is manufactured in China. Chinese crystal is marketed under several brand names, but in all cases, it contains only 20 percent lead. The lower lead content and mass-production manufacturing process produce lower-quality crystal beads that are lighter and less reflective than their more expensive counterparts.

# GEMSTONES

GEMSTONES ARE THE NATURALLY occurring crystalline forms of various minerals found in the earth's crust. They come in an enormous variety of colors and clarities and are grouped into families based on their crystal structure, chemical composition, and impurity content. The value of a gemstone depends on its beauty, its rarity, its clarity, and the way it is cut and polished. Traditionally, diamonds, emeralds, rubies, and sapphires have been considered the most precious gemstones and have commanded the highest prices in the marketplace. However, as other colored gemstones such as turquoise become increasingly rare, their prices have grown steadily.

Many other gemstones, including varieties of feldspar, garnet, and quartz, are sometimes referred to as "semiprecious" because they are more abundant and tend to be less expensive.

Today it is preferable to refer to all jewelry-grade stones as gemstones, regardless of their value.

Another significant way that gemstones are categorized is by their hardness, or scratch resistance. In the early nineteenth century, a system for identifying minerals had not yet been developed. In 1812, German mineralogist Friedrich Mohs developed a comparison scale of hardness to classify minerals by their physical characteristics rather than their chemical composition. This scale is still used today (see appendix).

The natural world produces a stunning array of minerals that transform into gemstone beads when cut, polished, and drilled. The following list represents only the most common gemstones; there are many more.

**Agate** and **jasper** are both chalcedony, a subfamily of quartz, and they share similar mineral content. Both form in volcanic rock and come in a vast range of colors that result from their varying mineral contents. The primary visual difference between them is that agate is translucent and jasper is opaque.

Agates generally have a fibrous, milky, translucent appearance with banded inclusions. Some common varieties of agate include *black onyx*, a very popular stone; *fire agate*, which ranges in color from white to deep orange with feathery banding; and *blue lace agate*, which ranges from light blue to deep blue with complex white banding.

Jaspers are opaque stones of virtually any color that have a grainy appearance with spotted inclusions. The spotting results from the particular way sediments settle in the volcanic rock as it cools. There are numerous varieties of jasper, including *picture jasper,* which is sand colored with dark, spotted or swirled inclusions; *silver leaf jasper,* which is pale gray with spotted swirls of white to dark gray; and *Madagascar jasper,* which is green with distinctive circular spotting in whites and pale greens.

**Feldspar** is the most abundant rock found in the earth's crust. Types of gemstone-quality feldspar include *amazonite, labradorite, moonstone,* and *sunstone.* These gemstones all have a fiery or "floating light" aspect because alternating layers of two kinds of feldspar shatter light as it is reflected.

**Garnet** has a crystal structure similar to gemstone-quality feldspar. Though typically thought of as deep red, only *pyrope,* the most common garnet, is that color. Garnet also comes in a range of other colors due to the slightly different chemical compositions of each gemstone. *Rhodolite* is purple-pink, *spessartite* is deep orange, *hessonite* is brownish red, *grossularite* is yellow-green, and *tsavorite* is deep green.

**Jade** actually refers to two distinct mineral gemstones — *nephrite* and *jadeite.* Due to their toughness, jades were used by early man to make axe heads, knives, and other weapons. Nephrite is always either creamy white or pale yellow-green. Jadeite comes in a full range of colors from white to brilliant green. The greater the content of iron in these stones, the greener they are.

**Precious gemstones** have been prized throughout history for their rarity and beauty and, accordingly, command higher prices. *Diamonds* have always been one of the most valuable and sought-after gemstones. They are remarkable for the way their crystal structure can split white light into the full spectrum of colors.

*Emerald* ranges in color from yellow-green to blue-green, with the most common hue being brilliant "emerald" green. The green coloration results from trace amounts of chromium in the stone.

*Sapphire*, while most commonly blue, can be found in a wide range of colors including pink, orange, and yellow.

*Ruby* in a deep, natural red is the most prized, but lighter shades also occur. Ruby is frequently heavily dyed to achieve that sought-after red color.

**Quartz** is the second-most-abundant rock forming the earth's crust. There are two types of quartz: those in which the crystal formation can be seen with the naked eye (macrocrystalline), and those in which the crystal formation can be seen only under high magnification (microcrystalline).

A common type of macrocrystalline quartz that forms as visible crystals is the gemstone *amethyst*, which is a transparent deep purple. The darker the purple coloration, the more valuable the amethyst is. *Citrine*, which is similar to amethyst in structure ranges in color from pale yellow to brown. Amethyst and citrine sometimes grow in the same crystal and form another gemstone called *ametrine*.

The transparent, colorless variety of quartz is called *rock crystal* or *crystal quartz*. Many consider this type to be the ideal form of quartz. *Rose quartz* ranges from pale pink to rose-pink and is one of the most popular quartz gemstones. Even though rose quartz tends to be fairly cloudy, it remains one of the more affordable gemstones. *Smoky quartz* ranges in color from pale gray to deep brown and is frequently treated with heat to enhance the depth of the brown coloration.

Other common varieties of quartz have a microcrystalline structure that is only visible under high magnification. *Aventurine* is a translucent green quartz gemstone with a grainy structure. The mineral inclusions in aventurine give it a special shimmering effect. *Carnelian* is a translucent, bright orange to deep red gemstone with a sheen that can be enhanced by polishing. *Tiger's eye* also has a fine sheen when polished but is noted for its parallel gold and brown stripes.

**Topaz** is a transparent gemstone that comes in a variety of colors. The color variations occur as a result of impurities in the stone. *Imperial topaz*, the most well-known variety, is pale yellow to golden brown. True blue topaz is rare, but varieties of pale gray stone are often heat-treated or irradiated to produce brilliant blue stones. Two common trade names for blue topaz are *Swiss blue topaz* and *London blue topaz*. *Mystic topaz* is a colorless or faintly colored topaz that is surface coated to produce a stunning rainbow effect.

**Tourmaline** is one of the most structurally complex gemstones found in nature and comes in at least 10 varieties. The color or combination of colors found in each stone is the result of where it was mined and the combination of elements found in the gemstone. Colors range from pink to red, from blue to green, and from brown and to black. Iron-rich tourmalines are usually black to deep brown, while magnesium-rich tourmalines are brown to yellow, and lithium-rich tourmalines are almost any color, including blue, green, red, yellow, and pink. Bicolored and multicolored tourmaline crystals are quite common. This occurs due to fluidity of the chemical content during crystallization. Tourmaline may be green at one end and pink at the other, or green on the outside and pink on the inside; this type is called *watermelon tourmaline.*

**Turquoise** is a comparatively soft gemstone that has been prized for centuries for its stunning, opaque blue-green color. The color of turquoise is determined by the chemical and impurity content of each stone and where it is mined. Good-quality stone has become harder and harder to find as the mineral has been overmined. Today the best turquoise is located in northeastern Iran. Other notable deposits are found in Afghanistan, Argentina, Australia, Brazil, China, Israel, Mexico, Tanzania, and in the southwestern United States.

Unfortunately, the value of turquoise has diminished because of treatments like stabilization (see page 29) and the introduction of imitation or synthetic turquoise-colored materials. Two stones that are frequently mistaken for turquoise are dyed *howlite* and dyed *magnesite.* If the price of turquoise is too good to be true, it is likely one of these imposters.

# METAL BEADS

METAL BEADS AND jewelry-making components (see Findings and Clasps, page 39) are made from a wide range of metals. Metals are generally categorized in three categories: precious metals, base metals, and hypoallergenic metals. In addition to metal type, a variety of metal beads are defined by the way they are made. Many metal beads, components, and findings (crimps, clasps, rings, and so on) are mass-produced, while artisans from around the world handcraft the finest metal beads and findings.

Various cultures around the world are known for the handcrafted metal beads that they have produced for generations. Small collectives of the Karen people in Thailand make gorgeous fine silver beads in traditional designs. These beads are referred to as Hill Tribe Silver Beads. Recently, due to the dramatic increase in silver prices, these collectives have begun producing their traditional designs in alternative metals, including brass and copper.

Indonesian Bali Silver Beads are made by silver workers renowned for crafting these expertly handcrafted sterling silver beads. The lost-wax method of casting metal beads continues in Ghana, West Africa, while Tibetan refugees in Nepal carry on their tradition of metal bead making. Nomadic tribes in Afghanistan continue their age-old tradition of creating metal beads, pendants, and amulets. Many contemporary artists and artisans are designing and producing beads and pendants in a range of metals, including copper, brass, and pewter.

Selecting a metal to use for your stringing project is a matter of personal preference, metal color, and cost. Precious metals include gold, fine silver, and sterling silver.

**Gold** is a soft, corrosion-resistant, easily worked metal. To improve durability and reduce cost, gold is produced as alloys with decreasing percentages of pure gold content. For example, 24-karat gold is 100 percent pure gold, while 14-karat gold is 58.5 percent pure gold. *Gold-filled* is a gold alloy combined with sterling silver or base metal in layers and then drawn or rolled into the desired thickness or shape. *Gold-plated* is typically copper electroplated with a thin layer of gold. *Vermeil* [ver-MAY] is 18-karat gold gilded or washed over sterling silver or another metal.

**Silver** is a lustrous, silvery white metal that is easily worked. Oxidation causes silver to patina or darken over time. *Fine silver* is .999 percent pure silver, whereas *sterling silver* is 92.5 percent pure silver and 7.5 percent copper. True sterling silver is always stamped .925. *Silver-filled* is a silver alloy that is drawn and shaped in a desired thickness and shape. *Silver-plated* is typically copper that is electroplated with a thin layer of sterling silver.

Base metals include nickel, nickel silver, copper, brass, and pewter.

**Nickel** is a silvery metal that is tough and corrosion resistant and easily molded. *Nickel silver* (also known as German silver or gun metal) is a silvery, hard, corrosion-resistant alloy of 65 percent copper, 18 percent zinc, and 17 percent nickel. There is no silver in nickel silver.

**Copper** is a reddish-brown, metallic element that is easily shaped.

**Brass** is an alloy containing 75 percent copper and 25 percent zinc, and **bronze** is an alloy containing 90 percent copper and 10 percent tin.

**Pewter** is an alloy containing 90 percent tin and 10 percent copper, antimony, and bismuth. *Britannia metal* is a pewter alloy that contains 92 percent tin, 6 percent antimony, and only 2 percent copper.

......................................................................................................................

# *Hypoallergenic Metals*

Hypoallergenic metals include stainless steel, niobium, and titanium. "Hypoallergenic" is a term coined by the cosmetics industry in the 1950s to indicate that certain products were less likely to cause an allergic reaction. Most people who have an allergy to metals are allergic to the nickel content of jewelry findings. Using nickel-free metals or alloys like gold, sterling silver, or niobium is the only way to avoid an allergic reaction entirely.

**Stainless steel** is a steel alloy that comes in hundreds of different grades. The most common steel alloy for jewelry findings is both stain- and corrosion-resistant and hypoallergenic. *Surgical steel* is a medical-grade, corrosion- and rust-resistant stainless steel.

**Niobium** is a soft gray metal with very low toxicity that is both nickel- and lead-free. Niobium findings are made in fun colors, as well as black and shades of copper and bronze.

**Titanium** is a very strong metal most commonly used for body jewelry and surgical implants. It is particularly useful for people with severe nickel allergies.

......................................................................................................................

# NATURAL BEADS

NATURAL BEADS ARE MADE FROM an amazing array of materials that include pearls, coral amber, wood, bone, seeds, and shells. The earliest known beads are over 100,000 years old and correlate with the emergence of modern human culture. These early examples of personal adornment are simple shells with hand-bored holes and a hand-painted coating of red ochre.

Certain fine materials like pearl, coral, and amber are considered by many to be organic precious gemstones. They are classified with other gemstones because of their unique beauty and because they are rare or costly to culture or harvest.

**Freshwater pearls** are most frequently used for stringing necklaces and bracelets. Cultured freshwater pearls are created by seeding the freshwater mussel with tiny beads of shell and allowing the mollusk to react to these irritants by excreting a substance called nacre. Over time the nacre builds up and lustrous pearls can be harvested.

**Coral** is formed by a huge colony of tiny sea organisms called coral polyps that build protective calcium carbonate skeletons. Over long spans of time, these colonies grow large enough to become coral reefs. Many species of coral are endangered, so today only certain species of coral may be harvested legally.

**Amber** is the fossilized resin from long extinct coniferous trees. True fossilized amber is very hard, sometimes has extinct insects encased in it, and does not crack or melt. Copal is a tropical tree resin from living trees that have not completed the fossilization process. It is often mistaken for amber but is less hard than true fossilized amber and will crack and melt.

**Nuts, seeds, and shells** are abundant around the world and can easily be transformed into beads with the simple addition of a hole. A small sampling of nuts and seeds that are used as beads include kukui nuts, betel nuts, sibucau seeds, buri seeds, and palmetto seeds.

**Wood, horn, and bone** have been commonly used to make beads and buttons for decades. Most beads made from these materials today are either recycled or come from sustainable sources. Animal products come from the leftovers of food production, and wood products generally come from fast-growing tropical trees such as palm, bayong, tiger ebony, black ebony, and rosewood.

# PLASTIC BEADS

Plastic beads are made from materials that are easily shaped and molded. Each type of plastic has its own recipe and unique properties.

**Lucite** is the brand name of a plastic developed by DuPont in 1931. The US military used Lucite extensively during World War II. After the war, DuPont marketed Lucite for decorative use including for beads and jewelry. Lucite beads made between the 1930s and the 1960s are some of the most beautiful. They were produced in fabulous colors, unique shapes, and often had unusual iridescent qualities.

**Resin beads** and other items are created through a multistep process. Resin is very lightweight, dyes easily, and can be both extruded and molded. Resin beads are often manufactured to mimic glass beads.

**Acrylic beads** are made from a variety of proprietary synthetic recipes and are frequently manufactured to imitate amber, crystal, and metal.

# BEAD TREATMENTS

MOST BEADS MADE FROM precious natural materials undergo further treatment to enhance their natural beauty. The practice of treating and enhancing gemstones and pearls has been going on for centuries. Gemstones and pearls are frequently heat-treated, irradiated, dyed, oiled, or stabilized to enhance their beauty or to alter their natural color. In fact, most gemstone and pearl beads available today have been enhanced in some way. Completely natural, untouched gemstones and pearls are very difficult to source and are consequently very costly.

**Heat treatment** is the oldest process of enhancement. Heat causes the color of a gemstone to lighten, darken, or change completely. It can also improve the clarity of a gemstone or produce an interesting surface luster. Soft materials like amber are treated at temperatures as low as 175°C for a few minutes, whereas hard gemstones like diamond, ruby, and sapphire are treated at temperatures as high as 1,800°C for several hours.

**Irradiation** bathes gemstones or pearls in radiation to enhance or totally transform the material's natural color. Sometimes irradiation is followed by a heat treatment to produce a better or new color.

**Oiling** is a process that reduces the visibility of micro-cracks and inclusions in soft gemstones, particularly emeralds. Gemstones are first soaked in cedar-tree oil and then heated under pressure to push the oil deep into the cracks and inclusions.

**Stabilization** infuses a porous stone like turquoise with a bonding agent to enhance its strength and prevent it from absorbing unwanted substances, like body oil, that can cause discoloration.

**Dyeing** is a process of soaking, or heating and soaking, beads in natural or chemical colorants to enhance or alter their color. Dyed beads are often apparent to the naked eye. The bead string may be colored, the bead holes may be darker than the rest of the bead, or the color of the bead may be incredibly unnatural.

**Coating** is a process equivalent to glazing beads with nail polish. Coatings are transparent chemical glazes, usually applied with heat, that increase luster or change the reflective quality of the surface of a bead. Some common coatings include the following:

- **Aurora borealis (AB)** gives a prismatic or rainbow reflection to the surface of a bead.
- **Vitrail** creates a pink-green surface reflection.
- **Luster** is a glossy coating that is used on glass beads in various color combinations, creating a popular effect.
- **Picasso** is a type of luster coating that produces a speckled, spotty finish that gives an earthy, natural appearance.

# CHAPTER TWO

# STRINGING MATERIALS

Stringing materials are the foundation of all strung beaded jewelry. Stringing materials are made from a wide range of materials from silk to steel. Popular choices include flexible beading wire, leather cord, silk thread, elastic, nylon, and rubber. Most stringing materials are available in a variety of diameters to accommodate a range of bead hole sizes. All of this variety allows for a great deal of creativity in designing bracelets and necklaces.

# FLEXIBLE BEADING WIRE

FLEXIBLE BEADING WIRE IS a strong, nylon-coated stainless steel beading wire. It is one of the most popular stringing materials used today. Clasps are easily and securely attached to this stringing material with crimp beads. The size and type of crimp beads used depends on the diameter of the flexible beading wire.

Two popular brands of flexible beading wire are SoftFlex and Beadalon. Both brands offer the best quality choices, in a variety of diameters, flexibilities, and colors. In addition to the standard silver, gold, and base metal colors, flexible beading wire comes in other colors, including black, white, and a range of seasonal fashion colors.

For most stringing projects, it is best to select the thickest wire that will fit comfortably through the beads being used. Different diameters of flexible beading wire are recommended for different sizes and weights of beads.

- **Very fine diameter** (.010 to .013 inch) is used with tiny, lightweight beads, gemstones, or pearls with very small drill holes.
- **Fine diameter** (.014 to .015 inch) is most commonly used for general purpose stringing projects. Light- to medium-weight beads, seed beads, crystals, and Czech glass beads string nicely on this diameter wire.
- **Medium diameter** (.018 to .019 inch) is best for medium-weight beads, large glass beads, stone beads, and for projects that need extra durability.
- **Heavy diameter** (.024 inch) is best used for projects that get a lot of use, like bracelets, lanyards, and eyeglass holders.

This diameter wire works best with large or heavy beads including lampwork, African trade beads, bone, and heavy stone. It is also appropriate for beads that have larger holes and that have rough or abrasive bead holes.

Another variable to consider when selecting flexible beading wire is the number of strands the wire is made with.

flexible wire

Beadalon produces a good-quality wire made with only seven strands of stainless steel. This is the least flexible wire they make. Both SoftFlex and Beadalon produce wires made with 19 or 21 strands of stainless steel that are stronger and more flexible. The best wires that SoftFlex and Beadalon produce are made with 49 strands of stainless steel wire, making them by far the strongest and most flexible.

## NATURAL STRINGING MATERIALS

EVEN THOUGH FLEXIBLE BEADING WIRE is very popular for stringing beads, some styles of jewelry or certain beads are better strung on natural stringing materials. The natural qualities of these stringing materials add an organic feel to jewelry strung on them. Popular cords made from natural materials include leather, cotton, linen, and silk.

**Leather** is a common option. The tanned hide is dyed and formed into round cord ranging in dimension from .05 millimeter to 5 millimeters. The most common sizes of leather cording are 1.5 millimeters and 2 millimeters and are used to string beads with 2 millimeter to 3 millimeter holes.

The finest-quality leather cording is made in Greece from cowhide. Lower-grade, less-supple leather cording comes from India and China.

Coil crimps are glued and crimped to the ends of the leather cording to attach a clasp.

**Suede** comes from the underside of cow or deer hide that has been stripped of the hard skin layer to leave a napped surface. Suede is dyed and then cut into a flat cord. Because suede does not have the tough outer layer, it is softer and less durable than leather cording. Suede is generally used with large beads that have large holes.

Fold-over crimps are used to attach a clasp to suede cord.

**Waxed cotton** is a thick, tightly woven cotton cord that is lightly waxed for durability. Waxed cotton comes in several diameters and is good for stringing beads with holes that match the diameter of the cord.

Both foil crimps and fold-over crimps can be used to attach a clasp to waxed cotton cord.

**Waxed linen** is a thin, tightly spun, linen cord that has a waxy surface that is applied for durability. Waxed linen comes in many colors and is popular for micro macramé and for stringing beads with smaller holes.

Bead tips can be added to the ends of waxed linen when adding a clasp.

**Hemp** is a strong, environmentally friendly fiber. Hemp is primarily used for macramé but can be used for stringing larger, organic beads. Hemp is manufactured in several thicknesses and is dyed in a complete range of colors.

Both foil crimps and fold-over crimps can be used to attach a clasp to hemp.

**Silk** is most commonly used for knotting between beads but can also be used to string small, lightweight beads. It comes in a variety of sizes or diameters appropriate for most sizes of beads and bead holes.

One of the most popular types of silk cord is *carded silk*. This twisted silk comes wrapped on a card with the beading needle already attached. Carded silk comes in sizes #0 (0.30 mm) to #16 (1.05 mm). Silk is also available on spools and is commonly used for longer knotting projects. Spooled silk comes in sizes 00 (0.012 mm) to FFF (0.419 mm).

Bead tips can be added to the ends of silk cord when adding a clasp.

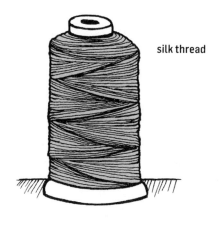

silk thread

# MAN-MADE STRINGING MATERIALS

FOR SOME PROJECTS, a man-made stringing material is the best choice. Cord, elastic, and ribbon made from man-made materials are very popular with those who prefer vegan options, for designs that require stretch, or for any application where a natural material is not suitable. Jewelry that will never be taken off or that is worn in the water frequently is often best strung on a man-made material for durability.

**Genya** is a round, synthetic leather stringing material. It is perfect for those who prefer a vegan stringing material or for jewelry that will be exposed to moisture on a regular basis. The most common diameters are 1 millimeter and 2 millimeters, which will fit beads with holes larger than 1 millimeter.

Coil crimps are used to attach a clasp to Genya.

**Elastic cording** is ideal for making stretchy jewelry projects. A clear, round type of stretch cord is used for stringing bracelets and anklets. It comes in three thicknesses and does not require the use of a beading needle. Clear round stretch cord can easily be finished with a square knot and a drop of strong glue.

Multistrand, flat stretch cord can be used for stringing bracelets and anklets, but requires a big eye or twisted wire needle to string beads with. Flat stretch cord can also be finished with a square knot and a drop of super glue or clear nail polish.

Cotton-covered elastic cord used in sewing clothing is useful for stringing heavier beads. The cord has an opaque elastic core that is covered with a tightly woven cotton cover. This type of elastic comes in a number of colors.

**Ribbon** comes in all sorts of materials and weaves including velvet, organza, grosgrain, and satin. This flat stringing material is particularly good for making simple flat chokers and bracelets.

Special ribbon crimps are used to attach a clasp to a piece of ribbon jewelry. For thin ribbon, bead tips or fold-over crimps can be glued and crimped when adding a clasp.

**Satin cord** is a round, synthetic silk cording that comes in a range of beautiful colors. It comes in 1 millimeter and 2 millimeter diameters and is used for simple stringing projects. One-millimeter satin cord is sometimes called "mouse tail," and 2 millimeter satin cord is sometimes called "rat tail."

Coil crimps or fold-over crimps are used to attach a clasp to satin cord.

satin cord

**Nylon cording** comes in several different varieties. The first is a bonded, no-stretch nylon thread that is popular for both stringing and knotting projects. The second is a 3-ply, twisted, multifilament nylon cording that is great for stringing, crochet, kumihimo, and micro macramé. This product comes in three weights: fine, medium, and heavy.

Bead tips are used to finish nylon cording when adding a clasp.

**Clear nylon cord** can be used for bead stringing, for creating illusion necklaces, and for off-loom weaving. This cord comes in several diameters to work with a range of bead hole sizes. Clear nylon cord can be knotted or crimped.

Crimp beads are used to attach a clasp to clear nylon cord.

**Rubber** is a waterproof stringing material that comes as both hollow and solid round cording. Common diameters of rubber cording are 1 millimeter, 2 millimeters, and 3 millimeters.

Coil crimps, fold-over crimps, or glue-on ends can be used to attach a clasp to rubber cording.

# CHAPTER THREE

# FINDINGS AND CLASPS

Once the beads have been strung, findings and clasps are added to finish the piece of jewelry so that it can be worn. These components secure the necklace or bracelet and add a professional finishing touch.

After the cord ends have been finished, most bracelets and necklaces require the addition of rings and a clasp so that the piece of jewelry can be put on and taken off with ease. Common types of findings and clasps include bead tips, crimps, jump rings, lobster claws, and toggles.

# BEAD TIPS, CRIMPS, AND ENDS

BEAD TIPS, CRIMPS, AND END CAPS are used to finish the ends of various stringing materials so that a clasp can be added. Each type of cord end is designed to work with a different style and diameter of stringing material. Bead tips are generally used with narrow diameter cords like silk and waxed linen, while coil crimps are used with larger diameter cords like leather and satin cord. Fold-over crimps are most frequently used with flat cords like suede.

**Bead tips** are used for holding and concealing the knots at the end of strung or knotted jewelry and for attaching a clasp to the end of a strung piece. The two common types of bead tips are *basket bead tips*, which look like tiny baskets with handles across the top, and *clamshell bead tips*, which look like a clamshell with a hook at one end. The clamshell bead tip closes over the knot to completely hide it.

**bead tips**

**Crimp beads** are tiny, tube-shaped metal beads that are compressed into small folds, or crimped, around flexible beading wire to secure each end of a clasp. Crimp beads come in several metals, sizes, and shapes.

**crimp beads**

**Crimp covers** are used to hide crimp beads at the ends of a piece of jewelry strung on flexible beading wire. They are for decorative use only and do not improve the strength of a piece of jewelry.

crimp covers

**Coil crimps** are coils of metal with a loop on the end that fits over and is glued to round stringing materials. A clasp and ring can easily be attached to the loop ends. Coil crimps come in a variety of metal colors to match clasps and other findings. They also come in several sizes to accommodate various diameters of round cording.

coil crimps

**Fold-over crimps** are U-shaped metal findings with a loop on one end. The sides of these crimps fold and are glued around flat or round stringing materials. A clasp can easily be attached to the loop end of the fold-over crimp with jump rings. Fold-over crimps come in a variety of metals to match clasps and other findings.

fold-over crimps

**Ribbon crimps** are jawlike metal findings with a loop at one end. Some ribbon crimps have teeth and others have smooth jaws. These crimps are clamped onto ribbon or other flat stringing materials and may be glued in place for added security.

ribbon crimps

**Glue-on ends** are used to hide thicker dimension cord ends and make a clean transition to a clasp. Glue-on ends are also called bullet ends, end caps, and barrel caps. Simply glue the cord into the end cap to attach a clasp.

glue-on ends

# RINGS AND CLASPS

EACH TYPE OF RING HAS a specialized use. They are made in a variety of metals, so they are easily matched to the other metals in your project. Each type of ring also comes in a wide range of sizes and wire gauges.

**Jump rings** are open, unsoldered rings that can be used to attach clasps, pendants, charms, and other components together or to a chain.

jump ring

**Soldered rings** are closed rings that can be used with crimped flexible beading wire, wire-wrapped pieces, or bead tips. Soldered rings are the most secure ring choice.

soldered ring

**Split rings** are small key ring–shaped rings that securely attach clasps and charms to chain or other rings.

split ring

As with rings, a myriad of different styles of clasps are available, from simple spring rings and lobster claws to more specialized closures such as tube and bar clasps. Selecting the best clasp for your project is partly a matter of taste, partly design, and partly application.

**Box clasps** are two-piece clasps with a box and a small, pressure-fitted piece that snaps into the box. Some box clasps have tiny snap locks for extra security. This clasp is good for use with bracelets and necklaces. Box clasps come in many shapes, sizes, decorative designs, and metals.

box clasp

**J-hooks** are J-shaped pieces of metal that connect with soldered rings or jump rings on either end. This clasp is best used on necklaces and comes in simple and decorative styles. J-hooks come in a range of sizes, designs, and in metals.

J-hook

**Lanyard clasps** are thin, one-piece clasps shaped like a long droplet with a flexible snap closure. This clasp is used mostly for ID lanyards or jewelry projects made on leather or hemp. Lanyard clasps are usually made from plated metals.

lanyard clasp

**Lobster claws** are very popular and secure clasps, frequently used with flexible beading wire and crimp beads. They can be used with just about any finding and stringing material to finish a jewelry project. This clasp is shaped like a lobster claw and comes in a variety of sizes, designs, and metals.

lobster claw

**Magnetic clasps** are two-part clasps held together by strong magnets. This type of clasp is good for lightweight jewelry and for people who have trouble opening lobster claws or spring rings. Magnetic clasps come in a wide range of magnetic strengths, sizes, and designs.

magnetic clasp

**Pearl clasps** are very traditional oval-shaped clasps with filigree detail. This type of clasp has a unique hook and snap closure that works best for necklaces. Pearl clasps used to be made only from precious metals but are now available in other metals as well.

pearl clasp

**S-hooks** are S-shaped pieces of metal that connect with soldered rings or jump rings on both ends. These clasps are best used on necklaces, and they come in simple and decorative styles. S-hooks come in a small range of sizes, designs, and metals.

S-hook

**Spring rings** are shaped like a ring with a spring-loaded barrel. This clasp is frequently used with flexible beading wire and crimp beads. A spring ring can also be used with just about any finding and stringing material. These clasps come in a variety of sizes and metals.

spring ring

**Toggle clasps** are made with two parts: a ring and a bar. The bar slides through the ring and then lies across it to close. This clasp is less secure than a lobster claw or spring ring but is often easier for the wearer to use, especially on bracelets. Toggle clasps are made in a vast array of decorative designs and are often included as a design element in jewelry projects. These clasps come in a variety of sizes, designs, and metals.

toggle clasp

**Tube and bar clasps** typically come with a bar and two, three, or five loops on each side of the clasp. The clasp component is made of two parts that slide together and snap into place. Some versions of these clasps are magnetic for added security. Tube and bar clasps are made from a variety of metals.

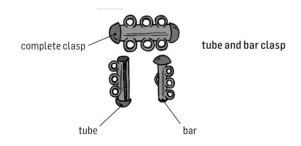

complete clasp

tube and bar clasp

tube

bar

# CAPS, CONES, AND SPACERS

Caps can be used to mask unsightly bead holes, cones may be used to hide the ends of a multistrand project, and spacers can add some sparkle or dimension to a bracelet or necklace. The addition of caps, cones, and spacers can also be a purely decorative design choice.

**Caps** are decorative, half sphere–shaped findings that fit over bead holes to disguise the opening or add to the design of the piece. They come in a complete range of designs, sizes, and metals from plated to precious.

caps

**Cones** are decorative, conical findings that are used to conceal multiple strands of beads attaching to a single clasp. They come in a complete range of designs, sizes, and metals from plated to precious.

cones

**Spacer beads** are decorative elements that are available in a multitude of sizes, shapes, and designs. A spacer bead is usually flat with a hole in the center, and it sits between round or shaped beads as another design element. They are used to add interest, sparkle, and pattern to any strung project.

spacer beads

**Spacer bars** are used with bar ends to make neat and orderly multistrand projects. The bars help keep the strands in order and help keep the piece flat when worn.

spacer bars

**Spacer bar ends** are used to transition multiple strands down to one for the ease of adding a clasp. Bar ends can be used with or without spacer bars.

spacer bar ends

# CHAPTER FOUR

# BEADING TOOLS

A jewelry maker's toolbox should be filled with a variety of beading pliers, cutters, and design tools. Each tool has a specific purpose. The three basic tools — round nose pliers, chain nose pliers, and side cutters — can be supplemented with specialty tools like crimping pliers and a split ring tool to round out a basic toolbox.

A bead board, measuring tape and caliper, and storage containers are also extremely useful. Good tools, proper technique, and lots of practice help produce professional results.

# BEADING PLIERS

Beading pliers and cutters range in quality from beginner tools, usually made in Pakistan, to intermediate tools made in Germany, to advanced tools made in Spain or the United States. The quality of the tools varies from the type of metal used to the way the tool is crafted. Some brands of beading pliers are spring-loaded, making them much easier to manipulate.

**Chain nose pliers** have a tapered jaw that is rounded on the outside but flat and smooth on the inside. This wire-working tool is commonly used for crimping and for gripping wire.

chain nose pliers

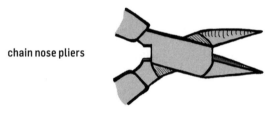

**Crimping pliers** are designed for crimping tube-shaped crimp beads into neat, folded crimps. This is an absolutely essential tool for the jewelry maker's toolbox!

crimping pliers

**Flat nose pliers** have a tapered jaw that is smooth and flat on both sides. This tool is useful for projects that require a larger gripping surface.

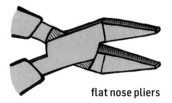

flat nose pliers

**Magical crimping pliers** transform 2 x 2 crimps into small round beads.

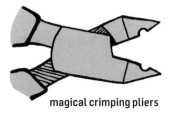

magical crimping pliers

**Round nose pliers** are beading pliers with a smooth, conical jaw for making loops. This beading tool is essential for making earrings or any wirework projects that have loops or curves. They are also useful for opening and closing bead tips. Round nose pliers should not be used for gripping.

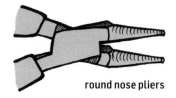

round nose pliers

**Split ring pliers** have a small tooth on one jaw that holds open a split ring while charms or another ring is fed onto the ring. This tool is especially useful for projects like charm bracelets.

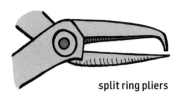

split ring pliers

# BEADING CUTTERS

IT IS USEFUL TO HAVE a variety of cutters on hand to cut through different stringing materials. Scissors or snips work for some materials, but cutters specifically designed to cut different metal materials are essential if you want to preserve the blades of your cutting tools.

**Flexible beading wire cutters** are flush cutters that easily snip through the nylon and metal layers of flexible beading wire. These cutters have small tips for precise cutting of delicate wires.

flexible beading wire cutters

**Side cutters**, or flush cutters, are an essential tool for cutting hard wire. The blades of a side cutter have a notched side and a flat side that allow for a close cut on small projects.

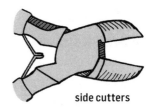

side cutters

**Snips** are small, thread-cutting tools that are useful for trimming the ends of nylon, silk, and elastic threads.

**Scissors** with long, narrow blades are an essential tool for cutting thread, elastic, or monofilament. The narrow blades allow for a close, accurate cut.

snips

# DESIGN AND SPECIALTY TOOLS

WHILE NOT ESSENTIAL, THE following items make it much easier to measure, design, and manage beading projects.

**Bead boards** are lightweight trays with channels for laying out bead designs before they are strung. The outer channels are marked off in inches and the inner channels in centimeters. Recessed areas on the bead board are ideal for keeping loose beads and findings in place. They are typically made of flocked plastic.

**Bead reamers** are used to open up or even out problematic bead holes. There are several varieties of reamers and bits available. Some are exclusively for pearls and others have interchangeable bits.

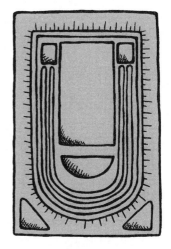

bead board

bead reamer bit

**Bead stoppers** are ingenious coiled clips that pinch on to the end of a stringing material to keep beads from accidentally falling off or spilling. Each bead stopper can hold several strands of stringing material at a time.

bead stoppers

## Tech Tip
*A simple knot or a piece of clear tape folded over the end of your stringing material can also be used to prevent beads from falling off. Other types of clips should be used with caution as they can bend, mar, or otherwise damage your stringing material.*

**Calipers** are small metal devices with a sliding jaw for measuring beads and bead holes. To use, slide open the jaw, place the bead in the jaw, slide the jaw closed, and then refer to the measurement guide to determine the size of the bead.

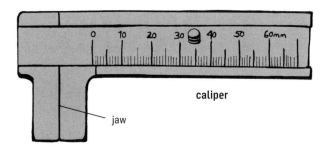

caliper

jaw

**Measuring tapes** marked in both inches and centimeters are useful tools. Beads are made in millimeter dimensions, but jewelry is frequently made in inches. Having a tape measure handy makes the conversion much easier.

**Storage containers** for beads, findings, and tools are essential: they protect your investment in materials, keep tools clean and sharp, and keep everything organized. A wide range of containers from screw-top stacking jars to flat compartmentalized boxes are available.

# CHAPTER FIVE

# JEWELRY PLANNING

Planning out your jewelry projects before you string them is a great way to save time and money. Research the styles of beaded jewelry you want to make by looking at magazines, books, and the Internet. Collect and save pictures of finished jewelry, interesting beads and findings, and colors or other visual information that inspires you. Your jewelry choices, just like your wardrobe choices, reflect your personality and your individual style. When you make jewelry you absolutely love, you will always feel confident.

Jewelry projects can be as simple or as complex as you like. A simple yet striking project can be made using a single size, shape, or color of bead or by combining just a couple of those design elements. A more complex design can be made by using graduated sizes of one shape of bead or by using a variety of bead shapes in a similar size. The most elaborate designs might incorporate a range of bead sizes, a variety of bead shapes and colors, and even multiple strands of beads.

Regardless of jewelry style, some practical matters always need to be considered first. Taking accurate measurements is essential. A piece of jewelry that is too tight can be bothersome to wear and if it is too loose, it can be easily lost. Calculating the quantity of beads and the correct length of stringing material needed before you shop will ensure you purchase enough beads and materials, and will help you control cost. Don't forget to figure spacers, clasps, and other findings in the overall length.

Finally, before you actually string your beads, it is very useful to plan out and arrange your beads on a bead board. This allows you to see your design and rearrange beads without wasting materials or spending time restringing.

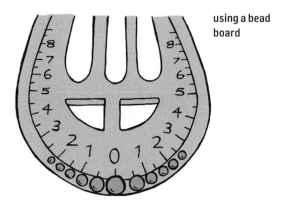

using a bead
board

# JEWELRY LENGTH

WHEN MAKING BEADED BRACELETS and necklaces, determining the proper length is very important. Whenever possible, measure the wrist or neck of the person who will wear the finished piece of jewelry. Even though there are standard bracelet and necklace lengths, each person has unique measurements.

Before making a bracelet, determine how tight or how loose the bracelet needs to be. Another factor is how many times it will wrap around the wrist. Measure the wrist of the person who will wear the finished bracelet with these things in mind.

With necklaces, length should first and foremost suit the wearer's neck measurement. There are six common necklace lengths to consider.

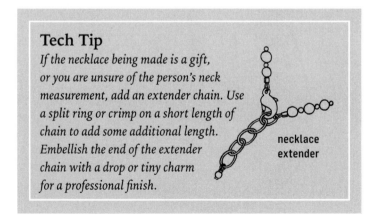

### Tech Tip

*If the necklace being made is a gift, or you are unsure of the person's neck measurement, add an extender chain. Use a split ring or crimp on a short length of chain to add some additional length. Embellish the end of the extender chain with a drop or tiny charm for a professional finish.*

necklace extender

## Common Necklace Lengths

**Collar length** is 12 to 13 inches long and made up of two or more strands that lie snugly in the middle of the neck. Collar-style necklaces are a wonderful complement to boatneck, V-neck, or off-the-shoulder fashions.

**Choker length** is 14 to 16 inches long and worn just above the collarbone. This classic and versatile style is appropriate with anything from casual clothing to evening wear and complements most necklines.

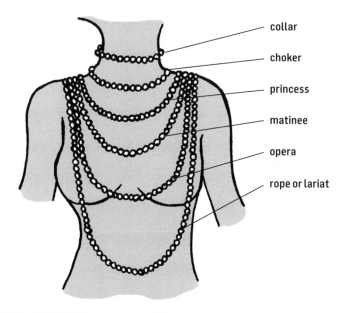

**THESE LENGTHS ARE** for an average adult woman and can be scaled up or down to best suit a person's neck size.

**Princess length** is 16 to 18 inches long and is one of the most popular lengths. Princess-length necklaces are great for crew necks or high necklines as well as plunging necklines. This choice is excellent if you are just not sure what length is appropriate.

**Matinee length** is 22 to 24 inches long and **opera length** is generally 30 to 32 inches long. Both options are versatile and attractive. These necklace lengths can be worn as a single strand with a high neckline or doubled and worn as a double-strand choker with moderate necklines. Opera-length necklaces were once only worn with formal evening wear, but today they are worn with any type of clothing.

**Rope or lariat length** is 45 inches or longer. This luxurious length is both elegant and dramatic. A rope-length necklace can be worn as one long strand or doubled or even tripled for a stunning and versatile look. Worn slung over one shoulder or down the back, it can also accent a backless dress.

**Bib style** refers to necklaces that are made from multiple strands of beads, with each strand longer than the strand above it.

Another thing to consider when deciding on necklace length is the neckline of the clothing that best suits it. Here are some common necklines and suggested necklace lengths to consider.

**Boatneck** necklines go straight across the collarbone, from shoulder to shoulder. Shorter necklace lengths are flattering with this neckline, especially ones with some substance.

**Button-up** collared shirts are a classic style that look great with a variety of necklace lengths. Wear a multi-strand necklace outside of the collar for a glamorous look, or add a short delicate necklace that peeks out from the collar for a subtle touch of sophistication.

**Crew neck** necklines are a classic, all-American style. Longer necklaces or layered necklaces work well with this neckline. Short necklaces tend to hide behind a crew neck collar.

**Scoop neck** necklines are very feminine, so delicate necklaces accentuate them nicely. Necklaces worn with a scoop neck tend to look best sitting at the collarbone or just below.

**V-neck** collars are distinctive. Layered strands and necklaces with pendants highlight the neck and collarbone. Make certain the necklace lands ½ to 1 inch above or below the base of the V, so the necklace does not hide behind the fabric.

**Embellished necklines,** including those with beading, ruffles, or lots of draping, don't really need any extra decoration. You may prefer to accessorize instead with a stack of bracelets or a pair of bold earrings.

# BEAD QUANTITY

As you prepare to shop for beads and supplies, it is helpful to first calculate how many beads you will need for a particular bracelet or necklace project. Bracelet sizes are determined by wrist measurement and bracelet style. Necklace lengths are determined by neck measurement, neckline style, and necklace style.

If you are shopping for strands of beads, the following Beads per Inch chart will help you determine approximately how many beads of a given size are on a strand of a given length. If shopping for loose beads, use the Number of Beads chart to help you determine how many beads of a given size you will need to create a given length.

## Tech Tip

*A retractable measuring tape or a caliper marked in millimeters is an essential tool for measuring bead dimension. It is always a good idea to have a measuring tool on hand when shopping for beads.*

## Beads per Inch

| BEAD SIZE | Beads per Inch (1 inch = about 25 millimeters) | | | | | | |
|---|---|---|---|---|---|---|---|
| | 1 INCH (25MM) | 6 INCHES (150MM) | 7 INCHES (175MM) | 10 INCHES (250MM) | 16 INCHES (400MM) | 18 INCHES (450MM) | 24 INCHES (600MM) |
| 2mm | 12 | 75 | 87 | 125 | 200 | 225 | 300 |
| 4mm | 6 | 37 | 43 | 62 | 100 | 112 | 150 |
| 6mm | 4 | 25 | 29 | 42 | 66 | 75 | 100 |
| 8mm | 3 | 19 | 22 | 31 | 50 | 56 | 76 |
| 10mm | 3 | 15 | 18 | 25 | 40 | 45 | 61 |
| 12mm | 2 | 12 | 14 | 21 | 33 | 37 | 48 |

## Number of Beads

| BEAD SIZE | Approximate Number of Beads Required | | | | |
|---|---|---|---|---|---|
| | BEADS PER INCH | 7-INCH BRACELET | 16-INCH NECKLACE | 24-INCH NECKLACE | 36-INCH NECKLACE |
| 2mm | 12 | 87 | 200 | 300 | 450 |
| 4mm | 6 | 43 | 100 | 150 | 225 |
| 6mm | 4 | 29 | 66 | 100 | 144 |
| 8mm | 3 | 22 | 50 | 76 | 112 |
| 10mm | 3 | 18 | 40 | 61 | 90 |
| 12mm | 2 | 14 | 33 | 48 | 72 |
| 16mm | 1 | 11 | 25 | 38 | 54 |
| 20mm | 1 | 8 | 20 | 30 | 43 |

# BEGINNING YOUR PROJECT

With all of your project materials and tools collected, create a comfortable, well-lit workspace for yourself. Select a comfortable chair that encourages good posture, choose a table or tray to place your jewelry-making materials on, and position good-quality task lighting over your work area. Reading glasses or lighted magnification can be useful when working with small beads.

No matter what type of stringing project you are planning, laying the beads out on a bead board will make your project go more smoothly. Each channel on the bead board is marked off in inches and millimeters, with zero being in the center front. Begin by deciding on the length of your finished project. Deduct the length of the clasp and any other findings that you are using to determine how many inches of beads you will need to lay out on the bead board.

Place your first bead at the center front (the zero mark) and add beads on either side of this center bead in whatever order or pattern you like. Lay out an equal number of beads on either side of the center bead until you have the correct length of beads in the channel of the bead board. For example, if you are making a 16-inch necklace and the rings and clasp measure 1 inch, you will need 15 inches of beads. Half of this total bead length (7½ inches) should then be laid out on either side of the center bead. Once you are satisfied with your design, you can string your beads using the appropriate technique.

# CHAPTER SIX

# STRINGING TECHNIQUES

Actually stringing the beads is the easy part. Finishing your strung jewelry requires learning some simple techniques for adding closures. This chapter includes a series of easy-to-understand, step-by-step instructions to help you finish your strung jewelry.

Projects made with flexible beading wire or clear nylon cord generally use crimp beads to attach the ring and clasp. Crimping involves tightly folding or compressing a crimp bead to secure rings and clasps to the ends of certain stringing materials. Projects made with round, flat, or large-diameter stringing materials generally use other types of crimp findings such as coil crimps, fold-over crimps, and ribbon crimps.

Mastering these techniques will help you complete different styles of jewelry, finish different kinds of stringing materials, and add different types of clasps.

## CRIMPING WITH FLAT NOSE PLIERS

Flat nose pliers are the best tool to use for flattening crimp beads of any size.

1. String a crimp bead and one side of a clasp onto the flexible beading wire.

2. Put the end of the wire back through the crimp bead so that it forms a loop through the loop of the clasp.

3. Use flat nose pliers to flatten the entire crimp bead. Check that the crimp is secure by pulling on the wire. Position the jaws of the flat nose pliers so that the entire crimp bead will be flattened when squeezed. Do not use the tips of the jaws to crimp.

4. String on a few beads, and tuck the tail end of the flexible beading wire through these beads. Clip the tail with wire cutters so that it is hidden in these beads. Use the flat side of the jaws of the wire cutters to get as close to the bead as possible. This placement of the cut will prevent the wire from poking the skin when the piece is worn.

5. String the rest of the beads, the second crimp bead, and the other side of the clasp. Put the end of the flexible beading wire back through the crimp bead and the last bead strung. Pull the tail to tighten the slack.

6. Use flat nose pliers to flatten the second crimp. Clip the tail with wire cutters.

## Tech Tip

*Hold the strung piece up in a gentle curve to ensure proper tension before crimping. If the piece is too loose, the flexible beading wire will be visible next to the crimp beads. If the piece is too tight, the piece will feel taut and not hang smoothly.*

## CRIMPING WITH CRIMPING PLIERS

Crimping pliers are the tool to use to create a folded crimp bead. Different crimping pliers are available to work with different sized crimp beads.

1. String a crimp bead and one side of a clasp onto flexible beading wire. Put the end of the flexible beading wire back through the crimp bead so that it forms a loop through the loop of the clasp.

2. Look at the jaws of the crimping pliers, and notice that the hollow closer to your hand is crescent shaped and the other hollow is circular in shape.

3. Center the crimp bead in the crescent-shaped hollow, and squeeze the crimping pliers firmly.

4. Move the crescent-shaped crimp bead to the circular hollow, and rotate it 90 degrees. It will now be sitting vertically in the jaw of the crimping pliers, with the curved (concave) side toward your hand. Squeeze the crimping pliers firmly to fold the crescent-shaped crimp bead in half.

5. String on the rest of the beads, the second crimp bead, and the other side of the clasp. Put the end of the flexible beading wire back through the crimp bead and the last bead strung. Pull the tail to tighten the slack (see Tech Tip below).

6. Use crimping pliers to secure the second crimp. Clip the tail with wire cutters.

## Tech Tip

*To be certain your crimp bead is secure pull gently on the flexible beading wire. If the wire slips, use flat nose pliers to compress the crimp a bit more.*

## USING A TUBE AND BAR CLASP

Tube and bar clasps are perfect for finishing multistrand necklaces and bracelets. They come with two, three, or five loops on each side of the clasp. The clasp component is made of two parts that slide together and snap into place. Some models are magnetic for added security. Use a crimping technique to secure strands to the loops or bars.

1. Slide the parts of the tube and bar clasp apart. Crimp the first strand of flexible beading wire to the top loop.

2. String the first strand to the correct length, and crimp the other end of this strand to the top loop of the other side of the tube and bar clasp. Before crimping, make certain the top loop of each side of the clasp is facing up. The tube and bar clasp only slides together in one way.

**3.** Crimp and string additional strands to the tube and bar clasp, as the design requires.

## Tech Tip

*Use a two-loop tube and bar clasp to make a four-strand necklace or bracelet by crimping two strands to each loop. Use a three-loop tube and bar clasp to make a six-strand necklace or bracelet, and so on.*

## USING COIL CRIMPS

1. Put a drop of super glue on the cord, and slide the cord all the way into the coil crimp. Let the glue dry for 1 minute.

2. Use chain nose pliers to gently squeeze the last coil of wire at the end of the coil crimp. Do not flatten the coil. Control the plier pressure so the coil crimp does not cut the cord.

3. Move the pliers around the last coil of wire at the end of the coil crimp, squeezing gently as you turn them.

4. Pull gently on the coil crimp to make certain it is firmly attached to the cord.

5. To open the loop on the end of the coil crimp to add a ring or clasp, grasp the side of the loop that comes off the top of the coil with flat nose pliers.

6. Use your fingers or another pair of flat nose pliers to push the open side of the loop away from the side of the loop being held by the pliers.

7. Slide a ring or one end of a clasp onto the loop. Close the loop by pulling the open side of the loop back towards the side of the loop being held by the pliers. Repeat on the other end of the cord.

## Tech Tip

*Do not pull the loop apart like opening a circle. This type of stretching weakens the metal.*

## USING FOLD-OVER CRIMPS

1. Put a dab of super glue on the cord, and slide it into the fold-over crimp. Let the glue dry for 1 minute.

2. Use chain nose pliers to firmly fold one side of the crimp down over the cord.

3. The fold-over crimp should now be secure on the cord.

**4.** Fold the second side of the crimp over the first.

**5.** Attach a clasp with a jump ring or split ring. Repeat this technique on the other end of the cord.

## USING RIBBON CRIMPS

1. Use a toothpick to place a thin line of super glue on the inside of a ribbon crimp.

2. Place the ribbon or flat cord inside the crimp and let it rest until the glue sets.

3. Use chain nose pliers to firmly squeeze the sides of the ribbon crimp together.

4. Attach a clasp to the loop of the ribbon crimp using a jump ring or a split ring. Repeat this technique on the other end of the ribbon.

## HOW TO OPEN AND CLOSE JUMP RINGS

Many pieces of strung jewelry use jump rings to connect the clasp. Putting on and taking off strung jewelry puts a lot of stress on the clasp and rings. Properly opening and closing a jump ring as you attach it is very important to maintaining the integrity of the metal.

1. Grasp the jump ring from one side with flat nose pliers.

2. Using your fingers or another pair of flat nose pliers, push one side of the loop away from the other.

3. Do not pull the loop apart as this will eventually break the wire. Your open jump ring should look like this from the side.

4. Slip on a chain, charm, or finding. Use the pliers to close the jump ring the same way you opened it. Move both ends of the ring or loop back and forth gently to close any gap.

## HOW TO USE SPLIT RING PLIERS

A split ring is a continuous double circle of wire coiled like a key ring. Split rings are sturdier than jump rings and are not likely to open accidentally. The split ring plier is a very handy tool for opening and holding split rings open.

split ring pliers

1.  Place the tip of the curved part of the jaw of the split ring pliers between the layers of the coil, near one of the ends. Squeeze down on the tool to open the coil.

2.  While holding the split ring open, slip a chain, a charm, or a clasp onto the end of the coil.

3.  Remove the split ring tool. Slide the chain, charm, or clasp around the coil until in moves freely around both coils of the split ring.

# APPENDIX

The Mohs Scale of Hardness was developed in 1912 by mineralogist Friedrich Mohs to compare hardness by seeing which gemstones could scratch others. On this scale, talc is the softest mineral and diamond is the hardest mineral.

## Mohs Scale of Hardness

| HARDNESS VALUE | GEMSTONE FAMILIES BY HARDNESS | GEMSTONE EXAMPLES |
|---|---|---|
| 1 (softest) | Talc | |
| 2 | Gypsum | |
| 3 | Calcite | Coral, pearl |
| 4 | Fluorite | Malachite, rhodocrosite |
| 5 | Turquoise | |
| 6 | Feldspar<br>Jade<br>Opal | Amazonite, fire opal, labradorite, moonstone |
| 7 | Garnet<br>Quartz<br>Tourmaline | Amethyst, citrine, aventurine, carnelian |
| 8 | Beryl<br>Spinel<br>Topaz | Aquamarine, black spinel, Swiss blue topaz |
| 9 | Corundum | Ruby, sapphire |
| 10 (hardest) | Diamond | |

# INDEX

Page numbers in *italic* indicate illustrations; page numbers in **bold** indicate charts.

# DON'T BEAD WITHOUT THIS BOOK!

Anyone who loves beading will have questions while learning new techniques, discovering new tools and tricks, and designing jewelry on their own. *The Beading Answer Book* covers everything from choosing supplies for a simple necklace to mastering the details of crocheting with beads. An indispensable reference, the book is filled with illustrated instructions and insightful advice to help all beaders solve their most vexing dilemmas.

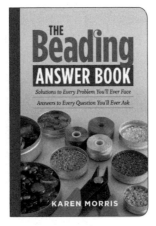

432 pages. Flexibind with cloth spine. ISBN 978-1-60342-034-1.